My Country
Egypt

Jillian Powell

A⁺
Smart Apple Media

Published by Smart Apple Media
an imprint of Black Rabbit Books
P.O. Box 3263, Mankato, Minnesota 56002
www.blackrabbitbooks.com

Published by arrangement with the Watts Publishing Group
LTD, London.

Library of Congress Cataloging-in-Publication Data
Powell, Jillian. Egypt / by Jillian Powell.
p. cm.—(My country)
Summary: "Hassan, a young boy from Egypt, introduces
readers to his country's landscape, weather, foods, and
festivals. Hassan also tells readers about his school,
family life, and things to see in Egypt. Includes a page of
facts about Egypt's population, geography, and culture"—
Provided by publisher.
Includes index.
ISBN 978-1-59920-904-3 (library binding)
1. Egypt—Juvenile literature. I. Title.
DT49.P69 2015
962—dc23
                2012042901

Series Editor: Paul Rockett
Series Designer: Paul Cherrill for Basement68
Picture Researcher: Diana Morris

Every attempt has been made to clear copyright. Should
there be any inadvertent omission please apply to the
publisher for rectification.

Picture credits: Albo/Shutterstock: 11; Atlaspix/
Shutterstock: 4b, 22c; Baloncici/Dreamstime: 5; Dan
Breckwoldt/Shutterstock: 2, 20; Tiziano Casalta/
Dreamstime: 8; Carlos Cazals/Corbis: 14; Jean Dominique
Dallet/Alamy: 15c; dbimages/Alamy: front cover c, 4t,
13b inset, 15b, 19b, 22t; David Forman/Latitudestock/
Alamy: 9t; Jeremy Graham/Alamy: 21; Janthon Jackson/
Dreamstime: 6; John James/Alamy: 12; Frans Lemmens/
Alamy: 19c; Christine Osborne/World Religions PL/
Alamy: 18; Ilene Perlman/Alamy: 17; PictureContact BV/
Alamy: 13; sculpies/Shutterstock: front cover r; slava296/
Shutterstock: 9b; Verdelho/Dreamstime: 7; Nickolay
Vinokurov/Shutterstock: 3, 10; Stuart Westmorland/
Corbis: front cover l; Zurijeta/Shutterstock: 1, 16.

Printed in Stevens Point, Wisconsin at Worzalla
PO 1654
4-2014

9 8 7 6 5 4 3 2 1

Contents

All words in **bold**
appear in the
glossary on page 23.

 Egypt in the World

My name is Hassan, and I come from Egypt.

Egypt is in two **continents**. Most of the country is in North Africa, but the eastern part is in Asia.

Alexandria

Cairo

Luxor

Egypt's place in the world.

I live in Cairo, which is
the capital city of Egypt.
It is the biggest city in
Africa and is always busy
with people and traffic.

Rush hour traffic
in Cairo.

People Who Live in Egypt

Fishermen on the Nile use nets to catch fish.

People in Egypt speak and write **Arabic**, but we often understand and speak English or French. Many people are Muslims, and some are Christians.

Most people live close to the Nile River where they can find work in the cities or in farming and fishing.

People have jobs in **tourism** and in factories that make oil, chemicals, cloth, and food products.

Tourists visiting the Great Pyramid of Giza.

Egypt's Landscape

Sand dunes in the Sahara Desert. The Western Desert is part of the Sahara.

Most of Egypt's land is **desert**.

The Nile River separates the Eastern and Western Deserts.

Farmland is mainly along the Nile River and the river **delta**. Farmers grow crops of cotton, sugar cane, rice, and oranges.

Farming by the Nile provides water for the crops.

The Red Sea coast is famous for its beautiful, sandy beaches.

Beach resorts are popular on the Red Sea coast.

9

The Weather in Egypt

The weather in Egypt is mostly hot and dry all year round. In April, hot dusty winds blow in from the Sahara Desert.

People riding camels through a desert storm.

The hottest months are in summer between June and August. Winters, from November to February, are usually mild and cloudy.

Sunset over the Nile.

At Home with My Family

I live with my family in an apartment in Cairo. We have a big living room at the front, a kitchen, a bathroom, and three bedrooms. My grandparents live a few blocks away.

we live on the ninth floor, so we have a good view over the city.

At home, I enjoy watching television or playing computer games. Sometimes, we go to the theater to see a movie.

Family is very important. Our cousins visit us a lot.

I like playing soccer with my friends.

What We Eat

In the evening, families sit down for a meal together.

At breakfast, we usually eat bread and honey or boiled eggs and some fruit.

The main meal is usually a spicy dish of meat or vegetables with rice and bread.

In the evening, we have **mezze**. These are different dishes and dips that we eat with flat bread, using the bread and our right hand to scoop up food.

Mezze can be made up of hot or cold dishes.

My favorite food is ice cream!

15

Going to School

Most children in Egypt start school at the age of 6. At primary school, we have lessons in math, reading, and writing.

We read Arabic writing from the right to the left on a page.

In the third year, we begin science lessons.

Muslim children, like me, also have lessons in the holy book of Islam, **the Qur'an.**

we read the Qur'an daily.

Festivals and Celebrations

We celebrate the first day of spring in March with picnics and boat trips on the Nile.

Street stalls along the Nile are busy during the spring festival.

Eid al-Fitr is an important Muslim festival. Families get together to feast and have fun after the month of **Ramadan**.

camel racing is a popular sport during Eid.

At Eid, we usually go to an amusement park.

Things to See

Many people come to see the pyramids at Giza. They were built for the **pharaohs** more than 4,000 years ago.

The pyramids are one of the seven wonders of the world.

People also like to take a cruise boat down the Nile River and visit the **bazaars** where they can buy rugs, bags, and jewelry.

The Great Bazaar in Cairo is very busy.

Here are some facts about my country!

Fast Facts about Egypt

Capital city = Cairo

Population = 83.7 million

Area = 386,622 square miles (1,001,450 km^2)

Main language = Arabic

National holiday = Revolution Day

Currency = Egyptian pound

Major religions = Islam, Christianity

Longest river = the Nile, 4,145 miles (6,670 km)

Highest mountain = Mount Catherine, 8,668 feet (2,642 m)

Glossary

Arabic the language of the Arab peoples

bazaars markets selling lots of different kinds of goods

continents main land masses of the world

delta flat land at the mouth of a river

desert dry area of land that gets little or no rain

mezze several small dishes of hot and cold foods

pharaohs kings of ancient Egypt

Ramadan ninth month in the Muslim calendar and when people fast (go without food) during the day

The Qur'an the sacred book of Islam

tourism industry serving visitors and holidaymakers

Further Information

Websites

http://news.bbc.co.uk/cbbcnews/hi/newsid_4090000/
    newsid_4096800/4096826.stm

www.kidcyber.com.au/topics/egypt.htm

www.touregypt.net/featurestories/children.htm

Books

Kalman, Bobbie. *Spotlight on Egypt (Spotlight on My Country).* Crabtree Pub., 2011.

Tracy, Kathleen. *We Visit Egypt (Your Land and My Land).* Mitchell Lane Publishers, 2013.

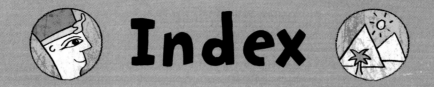

Index

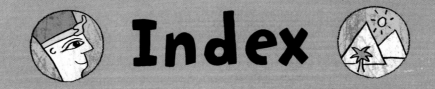

Index

Glossary

Arabic the language of the Arab peoples

bazaars markets selling lots of different kinds of goods

continents main land masses of the world

delta flat land at the mouth of a river

desert dry area of land that gets little or no rain

mezze several small dishes of hot and cold foods

pharaohs kings of ancient Egypt

Ramadan ninth month in the Muslim calendar and when people fast (go without food) during the day

The Qur'an the sacred book of Islam

tourism industry serving visitors and holidaymakers

Further Information

Websites

http://news.bbc.co.uk/cbbcnews/hi/newsid_4090000/
    newsid_4096800/4096826.stm

www.kidcyber.com.au/topics/egypt.htm

www.touregypt.net/featurestories/children.htm

Books

Kalman, Bobbie. *Spotlight on Egypt (Spotlight on My Country).* Crabtree Pub., 2011.

Tracy, Kathleen. *We Visit Egypt (Your Land and My Land).* Mitchell Lane Publishers, 2013.

Practical
Italian

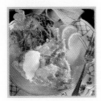

This is a P³ Publishing Book
This edition published in 2004

P³ Publishing
Queen Street House
4 Queen Street
Bath BA1 1HE, UK

ISBN: 1-40543-279-9

Printed in China

NOTE

Cup measurements in this book are for American cups.
This book also uses imperial and metric measurements. Follow the same units
of measurement throughout; do not mix imperial and metric.
All spoon measurements are level: teaspoons are assumed to be 5 ml, and
tablespoons are assumed to be 15 ml. Unless otherwise stated,
milk is assumed to be whole milk, eggs and individual vegetables such as potatoes
are medium, and pepper is freshly ground black pepper.

The nutritional information provided for each recipe is per serving or per person.
Optional ingredients, variations, or serving suggestions have
not been included in the calculations. The times given for each recipe are an approximate
guide only because the preparation times may differ according to the techniques used by
different people and the cooking times may vary as a result of the type of oven used.

Recipes using raw or very lightly cooked eggs should be
avoided by infants, the elderly, pregnant women, convalescents,
and anyone suffering from an illness.

Contents

Introduction

There are two main culinary zones in Italy: the wine and olive zone, which lies around Umbria, Liguria, and the South; and the cattle country, where the olive tree will not flourish—Emilia-Romagna, Lombardy, and Veneto—but where milk and butter are widely produced. Tuscany, however, is the exception: it uses both butter and oil in its cooking because both cattle and olive trees thrive in the area.

Italian food region by region

Piedmont: although the expensive fragrant white truffle is found in this region, and there is an abundance of exotic mushrooms, the food here is substantial, peasant-type fare. Garlic features strongly in the recipes, and polenta, gnocchi, and rice are eaten in larger quantities than pasta. A large variety of game is also widely available.

Lombardy: Milan is home to the marvelous risotto named after the city and also the Milanese soufflé flavored strongly with lemon. Veal dishes, including *vitello tonnato* and *osso buco*, are specialties, and other excellent meat dishes, particularly pot roasts, feature widely. The lakes produce a wealth of fresh fish. Rice and polenta are popular and pasta appears in many guises. The famous sweet yeasted cake called *panettone* is a product of this region.

Trentino-Alto Adige: here the foods are robust and basic, and fish are plentiful. In the Trentino area, pasta and simple meat dishes are popular, while in the Adige, soups and pot roasts, often with added dumplings and spiced sausages, are favored.

Veneto: polenta is served with almost everything here. The land is intensively farmed, providing mostly cereals and wine. Pasta is less in evidence, with gnocchi and rice more favored. Fish is in abundance and good seafood salads are widely available. There are also excellent soups and risottos flavored with the seafood and sausages of the area.

Liguria: excellent trattorias can be found all along the Italian Riviera: they produce amazing fish dishes flavored with the local olive oil. Pesto sauce flavored with basil, cheese, and pine nuts comes from this area, along with other excellent sauces, and fresh herbs abound.

Emilia-Romagna: tortellini and lasagna feature widely here, along with many other pasta dishes, and *saltimbocca* and other veal dishes. Parma is famous for its ham, which is called *prosciutto di Parma*. Balsamic vinegar is also produced here.

Tuscany: this region has everything: an excellent coastal area providing splendid fish, hills covered in vineyards, and fertile plains where every conceivable vegetable and fruit grow. There is plenty of game, providing many interesting recipes. Other dishes include tripe cooked in a thick tomato sauce, liver recipes, beans in many guises, pot roasts, steaks, and full-bodied soups. Florence has a wide variety of specialties, while Siena boasts the famous candied fruit cake called *Panforte di Siena*.

Umbria/Marche: inland Umbria is famous for its pork, and the cuisine is marked by the use of the local fresh ingredients, including lamb, game, and fish from the lakes. Spit-roasting and broiling are popular, and the excellent local olive oil is used in cooking and to pour over dishes before serving. Black truffles, olives, fruit, and herbs are plentiful and feature in many recipes. First-class sausages and cured pork come from the Marche, and pasta features all over the region.

Lazio: here there are many pasta dishes with delicious sauces, gnocchi in various forms, and plenty of dishes featuring lamb, veal, and other meats, all with plenty of herbs and seasonings. Vegetables and marvelous fruits are a feature, and beans appear in soups and other dishes.

Abruzzi and Molise: the cuisine here is deeply traditional, with local hams and cheeses from the mountains, interesting sausages with plenty of garlic and other seasonings, cured meats, and marvelous fish and seafood. Lamb features widely: tender, juicy, and flavored with herbs.

Campania: Naples is the home of pasta dishes, served with a splendid tomato sauce (with many variations). Pizza is said to have been created in Naples. Fish abounds, with *fritto misto* and *fritto pesce* being great favorites. Fish stews are robust and varied and shellfish are often served with pasta. Cutlets and steaks are excellent, served with

strong sauces flavored with garlic, tomatoes, and herbs; pizzaiola steak is one of the favorites. Mozzarella cheese is produced locally and used to create the crispy Mozzarella in Carozza, again served with a tomato sauce. Sweet dishes are popular too, often with flaky pastry and ricotta cheese, and the seasonal fruit salads are laced with wine or liqueur.

Puglia (Apulia): this region is stony but produces good fruit, olives, vegetables, and herbs, and there is plenty of seafood from the sea. Many excellent pasta dishes are exclusive to the region, both in shape and ingredients. Mushrooms abound and are always added to the local pizzas. It is not all fish or pasta, however: lamb and veal are roasted and stewed to perfection here.

Basilicata: potent wines are produced here to accompany a robust cuisine largely based on pasta, lamb, pork, game, and abundant dairy produce. The salamis and cured meats are excellent, as are the mountain hams. Lamb is flavored with the herbs and grasses of the region. Marvelous thick soups—true minestrone—are produced in the mountains,

and eels and fish are plentiful in the lakes. Chiles are grown in this region and appear in many recipes. The cheeses are excellent, good fruit is grown, and interesting local bread is baked in huge loaves.

Calabria: this is where oranges, lemons, and olives flourish, and a profusion of vegetables, especially eggplants. Chicken, rabbit, and guinea fowl are often on the menu. Pizzas and mushrooms feature largely, and pasta comes with a variety of sauces including artichokes, eggs, meat, cheese, mixed vegetables, sweet bell peppers, and garlic. The fish is excellent too, especially fresh tuna and swordfish. Many desserts and cakes are flavored with anise, honey, and almonds, and figs are plentiful.

Sicily: the cuisine on this island is based mainly on fish and vegetables. Fish soups, stews, and salads are unlimited, including tuna, swordfish, and mussels. Citrus fruits, almonds, and pistachios are widely grown, and the local wines, including the dessert wine Marsala, are excellent. Meat is cooked slowly, or ground and shaped before cooking. Game is plentiful and is often cooked in sweet-sour sauces containing the local black olives. Pasta abounds again with more unusual sauces as well as the old favorites. All Sicilians love desserts and cakes, and Cassata and other ice creams from Sicily are famous.

Sardinia: the national dish of Sardinia is suckling pig or newborn lamb cooked on an open fire or spit. Rabbit, game, and other meat dishes are also popular. There is an abundance of fresh fruit, and top-quality sea bass, lobsters, tuna, mullet, eels, and mussels. Myrtle, a local herb, is added to everything from chicken dishes to the local liqueur, and evokes fond memories of the island.

KEY
Simplicity level 1–3 (1 easiest, 3 slightly harder)
Preparation time
Cooking time

Italian Escarole & Rice Soup

This is a simple Italian soup made with the slightly bitter green scarola, or escarole, a member of the endive family.

NUTRITIONAL INFORMATION

Calories 183   Sugars 2g
Protein ....4g   Fat 11g
Carbohydrate ...19g   Saturates 7g

15 mins   1¼ hrs

SERVES 4–6

I N G R E D I E N T S

1 lb/450 g escarole or endive

4 tbsp butter

1 onion, finely chopped

4 cups chicken bouillon

1 cup risotto rice

freshly grated nutmeg

2–4 tbsp freshly grated Parmesan cheese

salt and pepper

fresh herbs, to garnish

1 Separate the leaves from the escarole or endive. Rinse under cold running water and drain. Stack several leaves in a pile and roll tightly, then shred the leaves into ½-inch/1-cm ribbons. Continue with the remaining leaves.

2 Melt the butter in a large, heavy pan over medium heat. Add the onion and

cook, stirring occasionally, for about 4 minutes, until soft and just beginning to color. Stir in the shredded escarole or endive and cook, stirring frequently, for 2 minutes, until the leaves wilt.

3 Add half the bouillon and season to taste with salt and pepper. Lower the heat, cover the pan, and then simmer gently over very low heat for about 25–35 minutes, until tender.

4 Add the remaining bouillon and bring to a boil. Sprinkle in the rice, partially cover, and simmer over medium heat, stirring occasionally, for 15–20 minutes, until the rice is just tender but still slightly firm to the bite.

5 Remove from the heat and season with nutmeg and more salt and pepper if necessary. Ladle into bowls and sprinkle with Parmesan. Serve garnished with herbs.

COOK'S TIP

You can substitute ½ cup long-grain white rice for the risotto rice, but the round, risotto rice is slightly more starchy.

Italian Cream of Tomato Soup

Plum tomatoes are ideal for making soups and sauces because they are denser than other varieties.

NUTRITIONAL INFORMATION

Calories 555	Sugars 18g	
Protein 11g	Fat 32g	
Carbohydrate ... 60g	Saturates 19g	

15 mins   40 mins

SERVES 4

I N G R E D I E N T S

4 tbsp unsalted butter

1 large onion, chopped

2½ cups vegetable bouillon

2 lb/900 g Italian plum tomatoes, skinned and coarsely chopped

pinch of baking soda

8 oz/225 g dried fusilli

1 tbsp superfine sugar

⅔ cup heavy cream

salt and pepper

fresh basil leaves, to garnish

deep-fried croûtons, to serve

1 Melt the butter in a large pan, add the onion and cook for 3 minutes. Add 1¼ cups of vegetable bouillon to the pan, along with the chopped tomatoes and baking soda. Bring the soup to a boil and simmer for 20 minutes.

2 Remove the pan from the heat and set aside to cool. Puree the soup in a blender or food processor and pour through a fine strainer back into the pan, pushing it through with a wooden spoon.

3 Add the remaining vegetable bouillon and the fusilli to the pan, and season to taste with salt and pepper.

4 Add the sugar to the pan, bring to a boil, then lower the heat and simmer for about 15 minutes.

5 Pour the soup into a warm serving bowl, swirl the cream around the surface, and garnish with fresh basil. Serve immediately with deep-fried croûtons.

COOK'S TIP

To make tomato and carrot soup, add half the quantity again of vegetable bouillon with the same amount of carrot juice and 1¼ cups grated carrot to the recipe, cooking the carrot with the onion.

Minestrone

Minestrone translates as "big soup" in Italian. It is made all over Italy, but this version comes from Livorno, a port on the western coast.

NUTRITIONAL INFORMATION	
Calories 311	Sugars 8g
Protein 12g	Fat 19g
Carbohydrate . . .26g	Saturates 5g

🐘

🍲 10 mins 🕐 30 mins

SERVES 4

I N G R E D I E N T S

1 tbsp olive oil

3½ oz/100 g pancetta ham, diced

2 medium onions, chopped

2 garlic cloves, crushed

1 potato, peeled and cut into ½-inch/ 1-cm cubes

1 carrot, peeled and cut into chunks

1 leek, sliced into rings

¼ green cabbage, shredded

1 celery stalk, chopped

1 lb/450 g canned chopped tomatoes

7 oz/200 g canned small navy beans, drained and rinsed

2½ cups hot ham bouillon or chicken bouillon, diluted with 2½ cups boiling water

bouquet garni (2 bay leaves, 2 sprigs rosemary, and 2 sprigs thyme, tied together)

salt and pepper

freshly grated Parmesan cheese, to serve

1 Heat the olive oil in a large pan. Add the diced pancetta, chopped onions, and crushed garlic and cook for about 5 minutes, stirring, or until the onions are soft and golden.

2 Add the prepared potato, carrot, leek, cabbage, and celery to the pan. Cook for another 2 minutes, stirring frequently, to coat all of the vegetables in the oil.

3 Add the tomatoes, small navy beans, hot ham bouillon or chicken bouillon, and bouquet garni to the pan, stirring to mix. Let the soup simmer, covered, for 15–20 minutes, or until all of the vegetables are just tender.

4 Remove the bouquet garni, season with salt and pepper to taste, and serve with plenty of freshly grated Parmesan cheese.

Mozzarella & Tomato Salad

Take advantage of the delicious varieties of cherry tomatoes that are available to make a refreshing Italian-style salad with lots of eye appeal.

NUTRITIONAL INFORMATION

Calories 295	Sugars 3g	
Protein 9g	Fat 27g	
Carbohydrate 3g	Saturates 7g	

4¼ hrs   0 mins

SERVES 4–6

I N G R E D I E N T S

1 lb/450 g cherry tomatoes

4 scallions

½ cup extra-virgin olive oil

2 tbsp balsamic vinegar

7 oz/200 g buffalo mozzarella (see Cook's Tip), cut into cubes

½ cup fresh flatleaf parsley

1 cup fresh basil leaves

salt and pepper

1 Using a sharp knife, cut the tomatoes in half and place them in a large bowl. Trim the scallions and finely chop both the green and white parts, then add to the bowl.

2 Pour in the olive oil and balsamic vinegar and use your hands to toss together. Season with salt and pepper to taste, add the mozzarella, and toss again. Cover with plastic wrap and chill in the refrigerator for 4 hours.

3 Remove the salad from the refrigerator 10 minutes before serving. Finely chop the parsley and add to the salad. Tear the basil leaves and sprinkle them over the salad. Toss all the ingredients together again. Adjust the seasoning and serve.

COOK'S TIP

For the best flavor, buy buffalo mozzarella—*mozzarella di bufala*—rather than the factory-made cow's milk version. This salad would also look good made with *bocconcini*, which are small balls of mozzarella. Look out for them in Italian delicatessens.

Tomato & Pasta Salad

Pasta tastes perfect in this lively salad, combined with onion and cherry tomatoes and dressed with wine vinegar, lemon juice, basil, and olive oil.

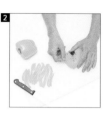

NUTRITIONAL INFORMATION

Calories 228   Sugars 4g
Protein . . . . .5g   Fat 12g
Carbohydrate . . .27g   Saturates 2g

50 mins   20 mins

SERVES 4

I N G R E D I E N T S

1½ cups dried pasta shapes

1 yellow bell pepper, halved and seeded

2 small zucchini, sliced

1 red onion, thinly sliced

4½ oz/125 g cherry tomatoes, halved

salt

sprigs of fresh basil, to garnish

D R E S S I N G

4 tbsp olive oil

2 tbsp red wine vinegar

2 tsp lemon juice

1 tsp mustard

½ tsp superfine sugar

handful of fresh basil leaves, torn into small pieces

salt and pepper

1 Cook the pasta shapes in a large pan of lightly salted boiling water for 8–10 minutes, or until tender but still firm to the bite.

2 Meanwhile, place the bell pepper halves, skin side up, under a preheated broiler, until they begin to char. Remove, place in a plastic bag, and tie the top. When cool enough to handle, peel off the skins and slice the flesh into strips.

3 Cook the zucchini in a small amount of lightly salted boiling water for 3–4 minutes, until cooked yet still crunchy. Drain and refresh under cold running water to cool quickly and prevent any more cooking.

4 To make the dressing, mix together the olive oil, red wine vinegar, lemon juice, mustard, and sugar. Season well with salt and pepper. Add the basil leaves.

5 Drain the pasta well and then tip it into a large serving bowl. Add the dressing and toss thoroughly to combine. Add the bell pepper strips, sliced zucchini and onion, and the halved cherry tomatoes, and stir to combine. Cover and set aside at room temperature for about 30 minutes to let the flavors develop.

6 Serve the salad garnished with a few sprigs of fresh basil.

Panzanella

This traditional, refreshing Italian salad of day-old bread is
ideal to serve for lunch or as a simple supper on a hot day.

NUTRITIONAL INFORMATION	
Calories 213	Sugars 11g
Protein 7g	Fat 6g
Carbohydrate . . .33g	Saturates 1g

45 mins   10 mins

SERVES 4–6

INGREDIENTS

9 oz/250 g day-old herb focaccia or
  ciabatta or French bread

4 large, vine-ripened tomatoes

5–6 tbsp extra-virgin olive oil

4 red, yellow and/or orange bell peppers

3½ oz/100 g cucumber

1 large red onion, finely chopped

8 canned anchovy fillets, drained
  and chopped

2 tbsp capers in brine, rinsed and patted
  dry with paper towels

about 4 tbsp red wine vinegar

about 2 tbsp balsamic vinegar

salt and pepper

fresh basil leaves, to garnish

1 Cut the bread into 1-inch/2.5-cm
cubes and place in a large bowl.
Working over a plate to catch any juices,
cut the tomatoes into fourths, reserving
the juices. Using a teaspoon, scoop out the
cores and seeds, then finely chop the
flesh. Add to the bread cubes.

2 Drizzle 5 tablespoons olive oil over
the mixture and toss with your hands,
until well coated. Pour in the reserved
tomato juice and toss again. Set aside for
about 30 minutes.

3 Meanwhile, halve and seed the
peppers. Place on a broiler rack, skin
side up, and cook under a preheated
broiler for 10 minutes, or until the skins
are charred and the flesh softened. Place
in a plastic bag, seal, and set aside for
20 minutes. Peel off the skins and finely
chop the flesh.

4 Cut the cucumber in half lengthwise,
then cut each half into 3 strips
lengthwise. Using a teaspoon, scoop out
and discard the seeds. Dice the cucumber.

5 Add the onion, bell peppers, cucumber,
anchovy fillets, and capers to the bread
and toss together. Sprinkle with the red
wine vinegar and balsamic vinegar and
season to taste with salt and pepper.

6 Drizzle with extra olive oil or vinegar
if necessary, but be careful not to let
the salad become too oily or soggy.
Sprinkle the fresh basil leaves over the
salad to garnish and serve immediately.

Pasta & Shrimp Parcels

This is the ideal dish when you have guests because the parcels can be prepared in advance, then put in the oven when you are ready to eat.

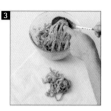

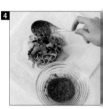

NUTRITIONAL INFORMATION

Calories 640	Sugars 1g	
Protein 50g	Fat 29g	
Carbohydrate . . .42g	Saturates 4g	

15 mins   30 mins

SERVES 4

INGREDIENTS

1 lb/450 g dried fettuccine

⅔ cup ready-made pesto sauce

4 tsp extra-virgin olive oil

1 lb 10 oz/750 g large raw shrimp, peeled and deveined

2 garlic cloves, crushed

½ cup dry white wine

salt and pepper

1 Cut out four 12-inch/30-cm squares of waxed paper.

2 Bring a pan of lightly salted water to a boil. Add the pasta, bring back to a boil, and cook for 2–3 minutes, until just softened. Drain and set aside.

3 Combine the fettuccine and half of the pesto sauce. Spread out the paper

squares and put 1 teaspoon of the olive oil in the middle of each. Divide the fettuccine among the squares, then divide the shrimp and place on top of the fettuccine.

4 Combine the remaining pesto sauce and the garlic and spoon it over the shrimp. Season each parcel with salt and pepper to taste and then sprinkle with the white wine.

5 Dampen the edges of the waxed paper and wrap the parcels loosely, twisting the edges to seal.

6 Place the parcels on a cookie sheet and bake in a preheated oven, 400°F/200°C, for 10–15 minutes, until piping hot and the shrimp have changed color. Transfer the parcels to 4 individual serving plates and serve.

COOK'S TIP

Traditionally, these parcels are designed to look like money bags. The resemblance is more effective with waxed paper than with foil.

Pasta Puttanesca

The story goes that this was a dish made and eaten by Italian women who needed a quick and simple meal to keep them going.

NUTRITIONAL INFORMATION

Calories	359	Sugars	........10g
Protein	........10g	Fat	..........14g
Carbohydrate	...51g	Saturates	.......2g

5 mins 25 mins

SERVES 4

I N G R E D I E N T S

3 tbsp extra-virgin olive oil

1 large red onion, finely chopped

4 canned anchovy fillets, drained

pinch of chili flakes

2 garlic cloves, finely chopped

14 oz/400 g canned chopped tomatoes

2 tbsp tomato paste

8 oz/225 g dried spaghetti

¼ cup pitted black olives, coarsely chopped

¼ cup pitted green olives, coarsely chopped

1 tbsp capers, rinsed and drained

4 sun-dried tomatoes in oil, drained and coarsely chopped

salt and pepper

1 Heat the oil in a pan and cook the onion, anchovies, and chili flakes for 10 minutes, until softened. Add the garlic and cook for 30 seconds. Stir in the tomatoes and tomato paste and bring to a boil. Simmer gently for 10 minutes.

2 Meanwhile, bring a pan of lightly salted water to a boil. Add the pasta, bring back to a boil, and cook for about 8–10 minutes, until tender but still firm to the bite.

3 Add the olives, capers, and sun-dried tomatoes to the sauce. Simmer for another 2–3 minutes. Season to taste.

4 Drain the pasta well and stir in the sauce. Toss thoroughly to mix. Transfer to a serving dish and serve hot.

Salmon Frittata

A frittata is an Italian slow-cooked omelet, similar to the
Spanish tortilla. Here it is filled with salmon, herbs, and vegetables.

NUTRITIONAL INFORMATION

Calories 300	Sugars 5g
Protein 22g	Fat 21g
Carbohydrate 7g	Saturates 8g

🍲 15 mins   🕐 1 hr

SERVES 6

I N G R E D I E N T S

9 oz/250 g skinless, boneless salmon

3 sprigs of fresh thyme

sprig of fresh parsley

5 black peppercorns

½ small onion, sliced

½ celery stalk, sliced

½ carrot, chopped

6 oz/175 g asparagus spears, chopped

3 oz/85 g baby carrots, halved

4 tbsp butter

1 large onion, thinly sliced

1 garlic clove, finely chopped

1 cup peas, fresh or frozen

8 eggs, lightly beaten

2 tbsp chopped fresh parsley

1 tbsp chopped fresh dill

salt and pepper

lemon wedges, to garnish

TO SERVE

crème fraîche or thick plain yogurt

fresh salad

crusty bread

1 Place the salmon in a pan with
1 thyme sprig. Add the parsley,
peppercorns, sliced onion half, celery, and
chopped carrot. Add water and bring to a

boil. Remove from the heat and set aside for
5 minutes. Lift out the fish, flake the flesh,
and set aside. Discard the poaching liquid.

2 Blanch the asparagus in boiling water
for 2 minutes. Drain and refresh
under cold water. Blanch the carrots for
4 minutes. Drain and refresh under cold
water. Drain again and pat dry. Set aside.

3 Heat half the butter in a large skillet
and add the remaining onion. Cook
gently for 8–10 minutes, until softened but
not colored. Add the garlic and remaining
thyme and cook for another minute. Add

the asparagus, carrots, and peas and heat
through. Remove from the heat.

4 Add the vegetables to the eggs with
the chopped parsley, dill, salmon, and
seasoning and stir briefly. Heat the
remaining butter in the skillet and return
the mixture to the pan. Cover and cook
over low heat for 10 minutes.

5 Cook under a preheated broiler for
5 minutes, until set and golden. Serve
hot or cold in wedges, topped with crème
fraîche or yogurt. Add some salad and
crusty bread; garnish with lemon wedges.

Corsican Clam Spaghetti

Fresh mussels can also be used to make this simple but delicious pasta sauce. Serve with a glass of chilled white wine.

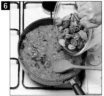

NUTRITIONAL INFORMATION

Calories 550	Sugars 10g	
Protein 25g	Fat 16g	
Carbohydrate . . .82g	Saturates 2g	

⏲ 50 mins   🕐 25 mins

SERVES 4

I N G R E D I E N T S

14 oz/400 g dried or fresh spaghetti

salt and pepper

C O R S I C A N
C L A M   S A U C E

2 lb/900 g live clams

4 tbsp olive oil

3 large garlic cloves, crushed

pinch of dried chili flakes (optional)

2 lb/900 g tomatoes, peeled and chopped, with juice reserved

½ cup green or black olives, pitted and chopped

1 tbsp chopped fresh oregano or ½ tsp dried oregano

1 To make the sauce, place the clams in a bowl of lightly salted water and set aside to soak for 30 minutes. Rinse them under cold running water and scrub lightly to remove any sand from the shells.

2 Discard any broken clams or open clams that do not shut when firmly tapped with the back of a knife. This indicates they are dead and could cause food poisoning if eaten. Set the clams aside to soak in a large bowl of water. Meanwhile, bring a large pan of lightly salted water to a boil.

3 Heat the oil in a large skillet over medium heat. Add the garlic, and chili flakes if using, and cook, stirring constantly, for about 2 minutes.

4 Stir in the tomatoes, olives, and oregano. Lower the heat and simmer, stirring frequently, until the tomatoes soften and start to break up. Cover and simmer for 10 minutes.

5 Meanwhile, add the spaghetti to the pan of boiling water, bring back to a boil, and cook until tender but still firm to the bite (8–10 minutes for dried spaghetti and 2–3 minutes for fresh). Drain well, reserving about ½ cup of the cooking water. Keep the pasta warm.

6 Add the clams and reserved cooking liquid to the sauce and stir. Bring to a boil, stirring constantly. Discard any clams that have not opened and transfer the sauce to a larger pan.

7 Add the pasta to the sauce and toss until well coated. Transfer the pasta to individual dishes. Serve immediately.

Pasta & Chicken Medley

Strips of cooked chicken are tossed with colored pasta, grapes, and carrot sticks in a pesto-flavored dressing.

NUTRITIONAL INFORMATION

Calories 609   Sugars 11g
Protein ....26g   Fat 38g
Carbohydrate ...45g   Saturates 6g

30 mins   10 mins

SERVES 2

INGREDIENTS

generous 1–1⅓ cups dried pasta shapes,
  such as twists or bows

2 tbsp mayonnaise

2 tsp bottled pesto sauce

1 tbsp sour cream

6 oz/175g cooked skinless, boneless
  chicken meat

1–2 celery stalks

4½ oz/125 g black grapes
  (preferably seedless)

1 large carrot

salt and pepper

celery leaves, to garnish

FRENCH DRESSING

1 tsp wine vinegar

1 tbsp extra-virgin olive oil

salt and pepper

1 To make the French dressing, whisk all the ingredients together, until smooth.

2 Bring a large pan of lightly salted water to a boil. Add the pasta, bring back to a boil, and cook for 8–10 minutes, until tender but still firm to the bite. Drain thoroughly, rinse, and drain again. Transfer to a bowl and mix in the French dressing while still hot, then set aside until cold.

3 Combine the mayonnaise, pesto sauce, and sour cream in a bowl and season to taste with salt and pepper.

4 Cut the chicken into thin strips. Cut the celery diagonally into thin slices. Reserve a few grapes for garnish, halve the rest, and remove any seeds. Cut the carrot into narrow julienne strips.

5 Add the chicken, celery, halved grapes, carrot, and mayonnaise mixture to the pasta and toss thoroughly. Taste and adjust the seasoning, adding more salt and pepper if necessary.

6 Arrange the pasta mixture on 2 plates and garnish with the reserved black grapes and the celery leaves.

Garlic Chicken Cushions

Stuffed with creamy ricotta, spinach, and garlic, then gently cooked in a rich tomato sauce, this chicken dish can be made ahead of time.

NUTRITIONAL INFORMATION

Calories	316	Sugars	. . . . .6g
Protein	. . . . .40g	Fat	. . . . .13g
Carbohydrate	. . . .6g	Saturates	. . . . . .5g

10 mins

40 mins

SERVES 4

I N G R E D I E N T S

4 part-boned chicken breasts

4 oz/115 g frozen spinach, thawed

¾ cup lowfat ricotta cheese

2 garlic cloves, crushed

1 tbsp olive oil

1 onion, chopped

1 red bell pepper, seeded and sliced

15 oz/425 g canned chopped tomatoes

6 tbsp wine or chicken bouillon

10 stuffed olives, sliced

salt and pepper

sprigs of fresh flatleaf parsley, to garnish

freshly cooked pasta, to serve

1 Make a slit between the skin and meat on one side of each chicken breast. Lift the skin to form a pocket, being careful to leave the skin attached to the other side.

2 Put the spinach into a strainer and press out the water with a spoon. Mix with the ricotta, half the garlic, and the seasoning.

3 Spoon the spinach mixture under the skin of each chicken breast, then secure the edge of the skin with toothpicks.

4 Heat the oil in a skillet, add the onion, and cook for a minute, stirring. Add the remaining garlic and the red bell pepper and cook for 2 minutes. Stir in the tomatoes, wine or bouillon, olives, and seasoning. Set the sauce aside and chill the chicken if preparing in advance.

5 Bring the sauce to a boil, pour into an ovenproof dish, and arrange the chicken breasts on top in a single layer.

6 Cook, uncovered, in a preheated oven, 400°F/200°C, for about 35 minutes, until the chicken is golden and cooked through. Test by making a slit in one of the chicken breasts with a knife or skewer to make sure the juices run clear.

7 Spoon a little of the sauce over the chicken breasts, then transfer to serving plates and garnish with parsley. Serve with freshly cooked pasta.

Chicken Risotto Milanese

This famous dish is known throughout the world—it is perhaps the best known of all Italian risottos, although there are many variations.

NUTRITIONAL INFORMATION

Calories	857	Sugars	.........1g
Protein	........57g	Fat	..........38g
Carbohydrate	...72g	Saturates	......21g

5 mins   55 mins

SERVES 4

INGREDIENTS

½ cup butter

2 lb/900 g skinless boneless chicken, thinly sliced

1 large onion, chopped

1 lb 2 oz/500 g risotto rice

2½ cups chicken bouillon

⅔ cup white wine

1 tsp crumbled saffron

salt and pepper

⅔ cup grated Parmesan cheese, to serve

1 Heat 4 tablespoons of the butter in a deep skillet and cook the chicken and onion until golden brown.

2 Add the rice, stir well, and cook over low heat for 15 minutes.

3 Heat the bouillon until boiling and gradually add almost all of it to the rice. Add the white wine, saffron, and salt and pepper to taste and mix well. Simmer gently for 20 minutes, stirring occasionally, and adding more bouillon if necessary.

4 Set aside for 2–3 minutes and, just before serving, add a little more bouillon and simmer for 10 minutes. Serve the risotto, sprinkled with the grated Parmesan cheese and the remaining butter.

Chicken & Tomato Lasagna

This variation of the traditional beef dish has layers of pasta and chicken or turkey, baked in red wine, tomatoes, and a delicious cheese sauce.

NUTRITIONAL INFORMATION

Calories 550	Sugars 11g	
Protein 35g	Fat 29g	
Carbohydrate ...34g	Saturates 12g	

20 mins   1¼ hrs

SERVES 4

I N G R E D I E N T S

9 sheets fresh or dried lasagna

1 tbsp butter, for greasing

1 tbsp olive oil

1 red onion, finely chopped

1 garlic clove, crushed

1½ cups mushrooms

12 oz/350 g chicken or turkey breast, cut into chunks

⅔ cup red wine, diluted with generous ⅓ cup water

generous 1 cup strained tomatoes

1 tsp sugar

B E C H A M E L   S A U C E

5 tbsp butter

generous ⅓ cup all-purpose flour

2½ cups milk

1 egg, beaten

¾ cup freshly grated Parmesan cheese

salt and pepper

1 Cook the lasagna in a pan of boiling water according to the instructions on the package. Lightly grease a deep ovenproof dish with butter.

2 Heat the oil in a pan. Add the onion and garlic and cook over low heat, stirring occasionally, for 3–4 minutes. Add the mushrooms and chicken and cook for 4 minutes, or until the meat browns.

3 Add the wine, bring to a boil, then simmer for 5 minutes. Stir in the strained tomatoes and sugar and cook for 3–5 minutes, until the meat is tender and cooked through. The sauce should have thickened, but still be quite runny.

4 To make the sauce, melt the butter in a pan, stir in the flour, and cook for 2 minutes, stirring constantly. Remove the pan from the heat and then gradually add the milk, mixing to form a smooth sauce. Return the pan to the heat and then bring to a boil, stirring, until thickened. Let cool slightly, then beat in the egg and half of the cheese. Season to taste with salt and pepper.

5 Place 3 sheets of lasagna in the bottom of the dish and spread with half of the chicken mixture. Repeat the layers. Top with the last 3 sheets of lasagna, pour over the sauce, and sprinkle over the remaining Parmesan. Bake in a preheated oven, 375°F/190°C, for 30 minutes, until golden and the pasta is cooked. Serve immediately.

Onion, Ham & Cheese Pizza

This pizza is a favorite of the Romans. It is slightly unusual because the topping is made without a tomato sauce base.

NUTRITIONAL INFORMATION

Calories 333   Sugars 8g
Protein . . . . .12g   Fat 14g
Carbohydrate . . .43g   Saturates 4g

🍳 1 hr   🕐 40 mins

SERVES 4

INGREDIENTS

1 tbsp olive oil, for greasing

1 large ready-made pizza base

TOPPING

2 tbsp olive oil

9 oz/250 g onions, sliced into rings

2 garlic cloves, crushed

1 red bell pepper, diced

3½ oz/100 g prosciutto, cut into strips

3½ oz/100 g mozzarella cheese, sliced

2 tbsp fresh rosemary, stalks removed, and coarsely chopped

1 Lightly grease a large cookie sheet with a little olive oil.

2 Place the ready-made pizza base in the center of the prepared cookie sheet.

COOK'S TIP

Prosciutto is an Italian, dry-cured, raw ham, said by many to be the best in the world. Other famous varieties of prosciutto include San Daniele and Veneto. This pizza would also be delicious made with Virginian Smithfield ham.

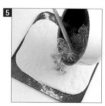

3 To make the pizza topping, heat the olive oil in a pan. Add the onion rings and crushed garlic and cook for 3 minutes. Add the diced red bell pepper and cook for 2 minutes.

4 Cover the pan and cook the vegetables over low heat for about 10 minutes, stirring occasionally, until the onions are slightly caramelized. Remove the pan from the heat and let cool slightly.

5 Spread the topping evenly over the pizza dough, almost to the edge. Arrange the strips of prosciutto, slices of mozzarella cheese, and chopped rosemary over the top.

6 Bake the pizza in a preheated oven, 400°F/200°C, for 20–25 minutes. Serve hot.

Tagliatelle with Meatballs

There is an appetizing contrast of textures and flavors in this satisfying family dish, which has now become known the world over.

NUTRITIONAL INFORMATION

Calories 910	Sugars 13g	
Protein 40g	Fat 54g	
Carbohydrate . . .65g	Saturates 19g	

45 mins   1 hr 5 mins

SERVES 4

I N G R E D I E N T S

1 lb 2 oz/500 g lean ground beef

1 cup soft white bread crumbs

1 garlic clove, crushed

2 tbsp chopped fresh parsley

1 tsp dried oregano

pinch of freshly grated nutmeg

¼ tsp ground coriander

⅔ cup freshly grated Parmesan cheese

2–3 tbsp milk

all-purpose flour, for dusting

3 tbsp olive oil

14 oz/400 g dried tagliatelle

2 tbsp butter, diced

salt and pepper

SAUCE

3 tbsp olive oil

2 large onions, sliced

2 celery stalks, thinly sliced

2 garlic cloves, chopped

14 oz/400 g canned chopped tomatoes

4½ oz/125 g sun-dried tomatoes in oil, drained and chopped

2 tbsp tomato paste

1 tbsp molasses sugar

⅔ cup white wine or water

1 To make the sauce, heat the oil in a pan. Add the onions and celery and cook until translucent. Add the garlic and cook for 1 minute. Stir in all the tomatoes with the tomato paste, sugar, and wine, and season to taste with salt and pepper. Bring to a boil and simmer for 10 minutes.

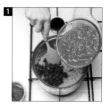

2 Meanwhile, break up the meat in a bowl with a wooden spoon, until it becomes a sticky paste. Stir in the bread crumbs, garlic, herbs, and spices. Stir in the cheese and enough milk to make a firm paste. Flour your hands, take large spoonfuls of the mixture, and shape into 12 balls. Heat the oil in a skillet and cook the meatballs for 5–6 minutes, until browned.

3 Pour the tomato sauce over the meatballs. Lower the heat, cover the pan, and simmer for 30 minutes, turning once or twice. Add a little extra water if the sauce is beginning to become dry.

4 Bring a large pan of lightly salted water to a boil. Add the pasta, bring back to a boil, and cook for 8–10 minutes, until tender but still firm to the bite. Drain the pasta, then turn into a warmed serving dish, dot with the butter, and toss with 2 forks. Spoon the meatballs and sauce over the pasta and serve immediately.

Spaghetti Bolognese

The original recipe takes about 4 hours to cook and should be left overnight to let the flavors mingle. This version is much quicker.

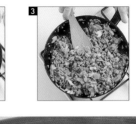

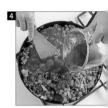

NUTRITIONAL INFORMATION

Calories 591	Sugars 7g	
Protein 29g	Fat 24g	
Carbohydrate . . .64g	Saturates 9g	

20 mins   1 hr 5 mins

SERVES 4

I N G R E D I E N T S

1 tbsp olive oil

1 onion, finely chopped

2 garlic cloves, chopped

1 carrot, scraped and chopped

1 celery stalk, chopped

1¾ oz/50 g pancetta or streaky bacon, diced

12 oz/350 g lean ground beef

14 oz/400 g canned chopped tomatoes

2 tsp dried oregano

½ cup red wine

2 tbsp tomato paste

salt and pepper

1 lb 8 oz/675 g fresh spaghetti or 12 oz/350 g dried spaghetti

1 Heat the oil in a large skillet. Add the onion and cook for 3 minutes.

2 Add the garlic, carrot, celery, and pancetta and sauté for 3–4 minutes, or until just beginning to brown.

3 Add the beef and cook over high heat for another 3 minutes, or until all of the meat is brown.

4 Stir in the chopped tomatoes, dried oregano, and red wine and bring to a boil. Lower the heat and let simmer for about 45 minutes.

5 Stir in the tomato paste and season with salt and pepper.

6 Cook the spaghetti in a pan of boiling water for 8–10 minutes, until tender but still firm to the bite. Drain thoroughly.

7 Transfer the spaghetti to a serving plate and pour over the bolognese sauce. Toss to mix well and serve hot.

VARIATION

Try adding 1 oz/25 g dried porcini, soaked for 10 minutes in 2 tablespoons of warm water, to the bolognese sauce in step 4, if you wish.

Veal Chops with Salsa Verde

This vibrant green Italian sauce adds a touch of Mediterranean flavor to any simply cooked meat or shellfish.

NUTRITIONAL INFORMATION

Calories 481	Sugars 1g
Protein 41g	Fat 34g
Carbohydrate 2g	Saturates 5g

🥩 10 mins ⏱ 5 mins

SERVES 4

I N G R E D I E N T S

4 veal chops, such as loin chops, about
  8 oz/225 g each and ¾ inch/2 cm thick

garlic-flavored olive oil, for brushing

salt and pepper

fresh oregano or basil leaves, to garnish

S A L S A   V E R D E

2 cups fresh flatleaf parsley leaves

3 canned anchovy fillets in oil, drained

1½ tsp capers in brine, rinsed and drained

1 shallot, finely chopped

1 garlic clove, halved, green core removed,
  and chopped

1 tbsp lemon juice

6 large fresh basil leaves or ¾ tsp freeze-
  dried basil

2 sprigs of fresh oregano or ½ tsp dried
  oregano

½ cup extra-virgin olive oil

1 To make the salsa verde, put the parsley, anchovies, capers, shallot, garlic, lemon juice, basil, and oregano in a blender or food processor and process until they are thoroughly chopped and blended.

2 With the motor running, add the oil through the top or feeder tube and process until thickened. Season with pepper to taste. Scrape into a bowl, cover with plastic wrap, and chill in the refrigerator.

3 Lightly brush the veal chops with olive oil and season to taste with salt and pepper. Place under a preheated broiler and cook for about 3 minutes. Turn over, brush with more oil, and broil for another 2 minutes, until cooked (test by piercing with the tip of a knife).

4 Transfer the chops to warmed individual plates and spoon a little of the chilled salsa verde beside them. Garnish the chops with fresh oregano or basil and serve with the remaining salsa verde handed separately.

COOK'S TIP

The salsa verde will keep for up to 2 days in a covered container in the refrigerator. It is also marvelous served with broiled red snapper.

Citrus Osso Buco

The orange and lemon rinds, together with fresh basil, give this traditional Italian dish a real southern flavor.

NUTRITIONAL INFORMATION

Calories . . . . .310 Sugars 4g
Protein . . . . .42g Fat 6g
Carbohydrate . . .16g Saturates 2g

15 mins   1½ hrs

SERVES 6

INGREDIENTS

1–2 tbsp all-purpose flour

6 meaty slices osso buco

2 lb 4 oz/1 kg fresh tomatoes, skinned, seeded, and diced or 1 lb 12 oz/800 g canned chopped tomatoes

1–2 tbsp olive oil

9 oz/250 g onions, very finely chopped

9 oz/250 g carrots, finely diced

1 cup dry white wine

1 cup veal bouillon

6 large fresh basil leaves, torn

1 large garlic clove, very finely chopped

finely grated rind of 1 large lemon

finely grated rind of 1 orange

2 tbsp finely chopped fresh flatleaf parsley

salt and pepper

1 Put the flour in a plastic bag and season with salt and pepper. Add the osso buco, a few pieces at a time, and shake until well coated. Remove and shake off the excess flour.

2 If using canned tomatoes, put them in a strainer and let drain.

3 Heat 1 tablespoon of the olive oil in a large, flameproof casserole. Add the osso buco and cook for 10 minutes on each side, until well browned. Remove from the pan.

4 Add 1–2 teaspoons more oil to the casserole if necessary. Add the onions and cook, stirring constantly, for about 5 minutes, until soft. Stir in the carrots and cook until softened.

5 Add the tomatoes, wine, bouillon, and basil and return the osso buco to the pan. Bring to a boil, then lower the heat, cover, and simmer for 1 hour. Check that the meat is tender by piercing with the tip of a knife. If not, continue cooking for 10 minutes and test again.

6 When the meat is tender, sprinkle with the garlic and lemon and orange rinds, replace the cover, and cook over low heat for another 10 minutes.

7 Taste and adjust the seasoning if necessary. Sprinkle with the parsley and serve immediately.

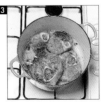

Gnocchi with Tomato Sauce

Freshly made potato gnocchi are delicious, especially when they are topped with a fragrant tomato sauce.

NUTRITIONAL INFORMATION

Calories 216   Sugars 5g
Protein . . . . .5g   Fat 6g
Carbohydrate . . .39g   Saturates 1g

30 mins   45 mins

SERVES 4

I N G R E D I E N T S

12 oz/350 g mealy potatoes, halved

⅔ cup self-rising flour, plus extra for dusting

2 tsp dried oregano

2 tbsp vegetable oil

1 large onion, chopped

2 garlic cloves, chopped

14 oz/400 g canned chopped tomatoes

½ vegetable bouillon cube dissolved in scant ½ cup boiling water

2 tbsp shredded fresh basil, plus whole leaves to garnish

salt and pepper

Parmesan cheese, freshly grated, to serve

1 Bring a large pan of water to a boil. Add the potatoes and cook for 12–15 minutes, or until tender. Drain and set aside to cool.

2 Peel and then mash the potatoes with some salt and pepper, the sifted flour, and the oregano. Mix together with your hands to form a dough.

3 Heat the oil in a skillet. Add the onion and garlic and cook for 3–4 minutes. Add the tomatoes and bouillon and cook, uncovered, for 10 minutes. Season with salt and pepper to taste.

4 Roll the potato dough into a sausage about 1 inch/2.5 cm in diameter. Cut the sausage into 1-inch/2.5-cm lengths. Flour your hands, then press a fork into each piece to create a series of ridges on one side and the indent of your index finger on the other side.

5 Bring a large pan of water to a boil, add the gnocchi, in batches, and cook for 2–3 minutes. They should rise to the surface when cooked. Remove from the pan with a slotted spoon, drain well, and keep warm while you are cooking the remaining batches.

6 Stir the basil into the tomato sauce and pour over the gnocchi. Garnish with basil leaves and season with pepper. Sprinkle with grated Parmesan and serve.

VARIATION

The gnocchi can also be served with a pesto sauce made from fresh basil leaves, pine nuts, garlic, olive oil, and romano or Parmesan cheese.

Pasta with Garlic & Broccoli

Here broccoli is coated in a garlic-flavored cream sauce and served on herb tagliatelle. Try sprinkling with toasted pine nuts to add extra crunch.

NUTRITIONAL INFORMATION	
Calories 538	Sugars 4g
Protein 23g	Fat 29g
Carbohydrate ...50g	Saturates 17g

5 mins   10 mins

SERVES 4

I N G R E D I E N T S

1 lb 2 oz/500 g broccoli

1⅓ cups garlic and herb cream cheese

4 tbsp milk

12 oz/350 g fresh herb tagliatelle

⅓ cup freshly grated Parmesan cheese

chopped fresh chives, to garnish

1 Cut the broccoli into even-size florets. Bring a pan of lightly salted water to a boil. Add the broccoli, bring back to a boil, and cook for 8 minutes, then drain thoroughly.

2 Put the soft cheese into a pan and heat gently, stirring constantly, until melted. Add the milk and stir over low heat, until well combined.

COOK'S TIP

A herb-flavored pasta goes particularly well with the broccoli sauce, but failing this, a tagliatelle verde or *paglia e fieno* (which means "straw and hay"—thin green and yellow noodles) will fill the bill.

3 Add the broccoli to the cheese mixture and stir to coat.

4 Meanwhile, bring a large pan of lightly salted water to a boil. Add the tagliatelle and bring back to a boil. Cook for 3–4 minutes, until tender but still firm to the bite.

5 Drain the tagliatelle thoroughly and divide among 4 warmed serving plates. Spoon the broccoli and cheese sauce on top. Sprinkle with grated Parmesan cheese, garnish with chopped chives, and serve immediately.

Exotic Mushroom Risotto

Distinctive-tasting exotic mushrooms, so popular in Italy, give this aromatic risotto a marvelous, robust flavor.

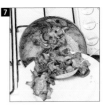

NUTRITIONAL INFORMATION

Calories 425   Sugars 2g
Protein . . . . .16g   Fat 17g
Carbohydrate . . .54g   Saturates 6g

35 mins   35 mins

SERVES 6

I N G R E D I E N T S

2 oz/55 g dried porcini or morel mushrooms

about 1 lb 2 oz/500 g mixed fresh exotic mushrooms, such as porcini, girolles, horse mushrooms, and chanterelles, halved if large

4 tbsp olive oil

3–4 garlic cloves, finely chopped

4 tbsp unsalted butter

1 onion, finely chopped

3 cups risotto rice

¼ cup dry white vermouth

5 cups simmering chicken bouillon

1⅓ cups freshly grated Parmesan cheese

4 tbsp chopped fresh flatleaf parsley

salt and pepper

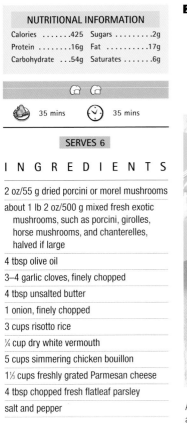

1 Place the dried mushrooms in a bowl and add boiling water to cover. Set aside to soak for 30 minutes, then carefully lift out and pat dry with paper towels. Strain the soaking liquid through a strainer lined with paper towels and set aside.

2 Trim the fresh exotic mushrooms and gently brush clean.

3 Heat 3 tablespoons of the olive oil in a large skillet. Add the mixed fresh mushrooms and stir-fry for 1–2 minutes.

Add the garlic and the soaked mushrooms and cook, stirring frequently, for 2 minutes. Transfer to a plate.

4 Heat the remaining oil and half the butter in a large, heavy pan. Add the onion and cook, stirring occasionally, for about 2 minutes, until softened. Add the rice and cook, stirring frequently, for about 2 minutes, until it is translucent and well coated.

5 Add the vermouth. When almost absorbed, add a ladleful (about 1 cup) of the bouillon. Cook, stirring constantly, until the liquid is absorbed.

6 Continue adding the bouillon, about half a ladleful at a time, letting each addition become completely absorbed before adding the next. This should take 20–25 minutes. The risotto should have a creamy consistency and the rice should be tender but still firm to the bite.

7 Add half the reserved mushroom soaking liquid to the risotto and stir in the mushrooms. Season with salt and pepper to taste and add more mushroom liquid if necessary. Remove the pan from the heat and stir in the remaining butter, the grated Parmesan, and chopped parsley. Serve immediately.

Pesto Pasta

Italian pesto is usually laden with fat. This version has just as much flavor, but is much healthier.

NUTRITIONAL INFORMATION

Calories . . . . 283 Sugars 5g
Protein . . . . .14g Fat 3g
Carbohydrate . . . 37g Saturates 1g

🄖 🄖

🄫 1 hr   🕑 30 mins

SERVES 4

I N G R E D I E N T S

3¼ cups sliced crimini mushrooms

⅔ cup fresh vegetable bouillon

6 oz/175 g asparagus, trimmed and cut into
   2-inch/5-cm lengths

10½ oz/300 g green and white tagliatelle

14 oz/400 g canned artichoke hearts,
   drained and halved

grissini (breadsticks), to serve

P E S T O

2 large garlic cloves, crushed

½ cup fresh basil leaves

6 tbsp lowfat plain yogurt

2 tbsp freshly grated Parmesan cheese

salt and pepper

T O   G A R N I S H

shredded fresh basil leaves

Parmesan shavings

1 Place the mushrooms in a pan with the bouillon. Bring to a boil, cover, and simmer for 3–4 minutes, until just tender. Drain and set aside, reserving the cooking liquid to use in soups if desired.

2 Bring a small pan of water to a boil and cook the asparagus for 3–4 minutes, until just tender. Drain and set aside, until required.

3 Bring a large pan of lightly salted water to a boil. Add the pasta, bring back to a boil, and cook until tender but still firm to the bite (8–10 minutes for dried tagliatelle or 2–3 minutes for fresh tagliatelle). Drain, return to the pan, and keep warm.

4 Meanwhile, make the pesto. Place all of the ingredients in a blender or food processor and process for a few seconds, until smooth. Alternatively, finely chop the basil and then mix all of the pesto ingredients together.

5 Add the mushrooms, asparagus, and artichoke hearts to the pasta and cook, stirring, over low heat for 2–3 minutes. Remove from the heat and mix with the pesto. Transfer to a warm bowl. Garnish with basil and Parmesan and serve with grissini.

Herb Focaccia

Rich with olive oil, this bread is so delicious it would
turn a simple salad or bowl of soup into a positive feast.

🄖 🄖 🄖

🔺 2 hrs   🕐 15 mins

MAKES 1 LOAF

I N G R E D I E N T S

3½ cups unbleached white bread flour, plus
extra for dusting

1 envelope rapid-rise dry yeast

1½ tsp salt

½ tsp sugar

1¼ cups lukewarm water

3 tbsp extra-virgin olive oil, plus extra
for greasing

4 tbsp finely chopped fresh herbs

polenta or cornmeal, for sprinkling

coarse sea salt, for sprinkling

1 Combine the flour, yeast, salt, and
sugar in a bowl and make a well in
the center. Gradually stir in most of the
water and 2 tablespoons of the olive oil to
make a dough. Gradually add the
remaining water, if necessary, drawing in
all the flour.

2 Turn out onto a lightly floured counter
and knead. Transfer to a bowl and
lightly knead in the herbs for 10 minutes,
until soft but not sticky. Wash and dry the
bowl and lightly coat with olive oil.

3 Shape the dough into a ball, put it in
the bowl, and turn the dough over.
Cover tightly with a dish cloth or lightly
greased plastic wrap and set aside in a
warm place to rise, until the dough has
doubled in volume. Meanwhile, sprinkle
polenta over a cookie sheet.

4 Turn the dough out onto a lightly
floured counter and knead lightly.
Cover with the upturned bowl and let
stand for 10 minutes.

5 Roll out and pat the dough into a
10-inch/25-cm circle, about ½ inch/
1 cm thick, and carefully transfer it to the
prepared cookie sheet. Cover with a dish
cloth and set aside to rise again for
15 minutes.

6 Using a lightly oiled finger, poke
indentations all over the surface of
the loaf. Drizzle over the remaining olive
oil and sprinkle lightly with sea salt. Bake
in a preheated oven, 450°F/230°C, for
15 minutes, or until golden brown and the
loaf sounds hollow when tapped on the
bottom. Transfer the loaf to a wire rack to
cool completely.

Peaches & Mascarpone

If you prepare these in advance, all you have to do is put the peaches on the barbecue grill when you are ready to serve them.

NUTRITIONAL INFORMATION

Calories . . . . . . .301 Sugars 24g
Protein . . . . .6g Fat 20g
Carbohydrate . . .24g Saturates 9g

🍲 10 mins   🕙 10 mins

SERVES 4

I N G R E D I E N T S

4 peaches

¾ cup mascarpone cheese

⅓ cup pecans or walnuts, chopped

1 tsp sunflower oil

4 tbsp maple syrup

1 Cut the peaches in half and remove the pits. If you are preparing this recipe in advance, press the peach halves together again and wrap them in plastic wrap, until required.

2 Combine the mascarpone and pecans in a small bowl. Set aside to chill in the refrigerator, until required.

3 To serve, brush the peaches with a little oil and place on a rack set over medium hot coals. Grill for 5–10 minutes, turning once, until hot.

4 Transfer the peaches to a serving dish and top with the mascarpone cheese mixture.

5 Drizzle the maple syrup over the peaches and mascarpone filling and serve immediately.

VARIATION

You can use nectarines instead of peaches for this recipe. Remember to choose ripe but firm fruit, which won't go soft and mushy when it is grilled. Prepare the nectarines in the same way as the peaches and grill for 5–10 minutes.

Balsamic Strawberries

Generations of Italian cooks have known that the unlikely combination of freshly ground black pepper and ripe, juicy strawberries is marvelous.

NUTRITIONAL INFORMATION

Calories	132	Sugars	.........5g
Protein	.........1g	Fat	..........12g
Carbohydrate	....5g	Saturates	.......7g

4¼ hrs | 0 mins

SERVES 4–6

INGREDIENTS

1 lb/450 g fresh strawberries

2–3 tbsp balsamic vinegar

fresh mint leaves, torn, plus extra to decorate (optional)

½–¾ cup mascarpone cheese

freshly ground black pepper

1 Wipe the strawberries with a damp cloth instead of rinsing them, so that they do not become soggy. Using a paring knife, cut off the green stalks at the top and use the tip of the knife to remove the cores or hulls.

2 Cut each strawberry in half lengthwise or into fourths if large. Transfer to a bowl.

COOK'S TIP

This is most enjoyable when it is made with the best-quality balsamic vinegar, one that has aged slowly and has turned thick and syrupy. Unfortunately, the genuine mixture is always expensive. Less expensive versions are artificially sweetened and colored with caramel.

3 Add the balsamic vinegar, allowing ½ tablespoon per person. Add several twists of freshly ground black pepper, then gently stir together. Cover with plastic wrap and chill for up to 4 hours.

4 Just before serving, stir in torn mint leaves to taste. Spoon the mascarpone into bowls and spoon the berries on top. Decorate with a few mint leaves, if using. Sprinkle with extra pepper to taste.

Italian Bread Dessert

This deliciously rich dessert is cooked with cream and apples and is delicately flavored with orange.

NUTRITIONAL INFORMATION

Calories	387	Sugars	........31g
Protein	.........8g	Fat	..........20g
Carbohydrate	...45g	Saturates	......12g

45 mins   25 mins

SERVES 4

I N G R E D I E N T S

1 tbsp butter

2 small dessert apples, peeled, cored, and sliced into rings

½ cup granulated sugar

2 tbsp white wine

4 thick slices of bread (about 4 oz/115 g), crusts removed (day-old baguette is ideal)

1¼ cups light cream

2 eggs, beaten

pared rind of 1 orange, cut into short, thin sticks

1 Lightly grease a 5-cup deep casserole with the butter.

2 Arrange the apple rings in the bottom of the dish. Sprinkle half of the sugar over the apples.

3 Pour the wine over the apples. Add the bread slices, pushing them down with your hands to flatten them slightly.

4 Mix the cream with the eggs, the remaining sugar, and the orange rind and pour the mixture over the bread. Set aside to soak for 30 minutes.

5 Transfer the dessert to an oven preheated to 350°F/180°C and bake for 25 minutes, until golden and set. Remove from the oven, set aside to cool slightly, and serve warm.